I0797735

UNION SQUARE KIDS and the distinctive Union Square Kids logo are trademarks of Hachette Book Group, Inc.

ISBN 978-1-4549-6168-0

Library of Congress Control Number: 2025024801

Union Square Kids books may be purchased in bulk for business, educational, or promotional use. For more information, please contact your local bookseller or the Hachette Book Group's Special Markets department at special.markets@hbgusa.com.

Printed in Guangdong, China

Lot #:

2 4 6 8 10 9 7 5 3 1

08/25

unionsquareandco.com

Text by Stephen Krensky
Book design by Ashtyn Botterill
Edited by Sarah Carpenter

For my grandchildren: Davis, Logan, Alex, and Leila.—S.K.

For Mum and Dad. Lots of love.—R.B.

FRIDA KAHLO

Written by Stephen Krensky
Illustrated by Ruth Burrows

How to use this book

In this book you'll find **ten genius stories** to read, each one just **5 minutes long**.

At the end of each story, explore an informative **"all about"** spread.

Want to learn more? Turn to the back of the book to discover a **timeline of key events**.

union square kids
NEW YORK

WHO WAS FRIDA KAHLO?

Frida Kahlo was a distinguished Mexican artist who mixed surrealistic elements with traditional painting techniques. She was especially known for creating emotionally revealing self-portraits. Follow her path to becoming a visionary artist.

THE CREATIVE SPARK

Young Frida suffers from an illness and finds ways to help recover her strength.

A BOLD FIGHT

As a teenager at school, Frida discovers many new political and social ideas.

TRIUMPH OVER TRAGEDY

After a terrible accident, Frida must spend many months in bed, where she kindles a new interest in painting.

SYMBOLS OF THE PAST

As Frida pursues a career in painting, she explores mixing different elements of Mexican culture into her work.

STORIES IN ART

Frida realizes that her art can combine different themes and go beyond copying images from life.

Page 48

AN ARTIST WITH PROMISE

Frida travels to different places in the United States while her art continues to evolve.

Page 58

THE TWO FRIDAS

After a show featuring her work, Frida must chart a new course for her personal and professional life.

Page 68

TEACHING LOS FRIDOS

Frida becomes a teacher. She takes an unconventional approach to help her students develop their potential.

Page 78

THE DEER IN THE WOOD

Frida struggles to continue her work while undergoing several operations to fight her chronic aches and pains.

Page 88

FRIDA'S LEGACY

Although Frida's health becomes more fragile, she still manages to host the first art show of her work in Mexico.

Page 98

WHICH 5-MINUTE GENIUS STORY WILL YOU READ TODAY?

THE CREATIVE SPARK

Frida Overcomes an Early Hurdle

Frida Kahlo was someone who looked at the world a little differently. She was born in Mexico on July 6, 1907.

Her father was a photographer and her mother ran their household. Young Frida loved to play in her room and dig in the garden.

But when she was six, everything changed. At first, she thought she had stubbed her toe. But soon she felt a terrible pain in her right leg. Her parents tried bathing Frida's leg in warm water to relieve the pain.

They soon learned that Frida's pain was because of a disease called polio. She would need medical care.

Some children who got polio never walked again. Many others died.

Frida spent the next nine months in bed. For a girl used to running and jumping, it seemed like forever.

Unfortunately, even when she got better, Frida was not entirely cured. Her right leg was now thinner and shorter than her left, and would stay that way. After that, Frida always walked with a limp.

Once Frida recovered, her doctor recommended that she play sports to regain her strength. Her father encouraged her, too.

At that time, girls did not play soccer or box, and it was considered unladylike for girls to ride bicycles or climb trees. But Frida was not like most girls.

Frida had missed a lot of school while she was sick. But going back to class wasn't easy. She felt embarrassed by the change in her appearance. Frida tried wearing extra socks on her right leg so no one would notice.

But everyone did notice. Many of the other kids made fun of her. They joked about her appearance. They called her "Pegleg."

Frida yelled at her classmates for calling her names. She tried to be tough. But she couldn't pretend the names didn't hurt. It had been bad enough to have been kept apart all those months when she was stuck in bed.

It was worse to still feel apart from everyone now that she was back on her feet.

Frida retreated into herself more and more. The pain in her leg never completely went away. She passed the time by helping her father with his photography.

He taught her how to develop photographs and later how to color them. This new hobby opened a whole different world for Frida.

Over time Frida raised up her head again. She had learned to depend on herself above all. If she could gain enough confidence, then it didn't matter what anyone else thought.

It only mattered what Frida thought of herself.

Photographic PORTRAITS

Helping her father with his photography was one of Frida's first creative experiences.

In the early 1900s, many professional photographers like Frida's father still used **large bulky cameras** mounted on tripods.

A tripod kept the camera from wobbling while the photograph was being taken.

The **shutter** on a **lens** was opened by hand to let light in. This light hit a sheet of **film** that caused a chemical reaction that left a print of the picture.

During this process—which lasted several minutes—the **subject** of the photograph needed to sit very still. It was easier to maintain a stiff or serious pose longer than a smile.

Working with her father taught Frida many things about **portraiture** that she would go on to use in her own art.

A BOLD FIGHT

Frida Learns to Speak her Mind

Frida Kahlo began to make a name for herself when she was a teenager. She was no longer a child, and she was ready to share her beliefs with the world.

In 1922, when she was fifteen, Frida was admitted to the famous National Preparatory School in Mexico City.

Outside of school, Frida spent time in fields and on riverbanks learning about nature.

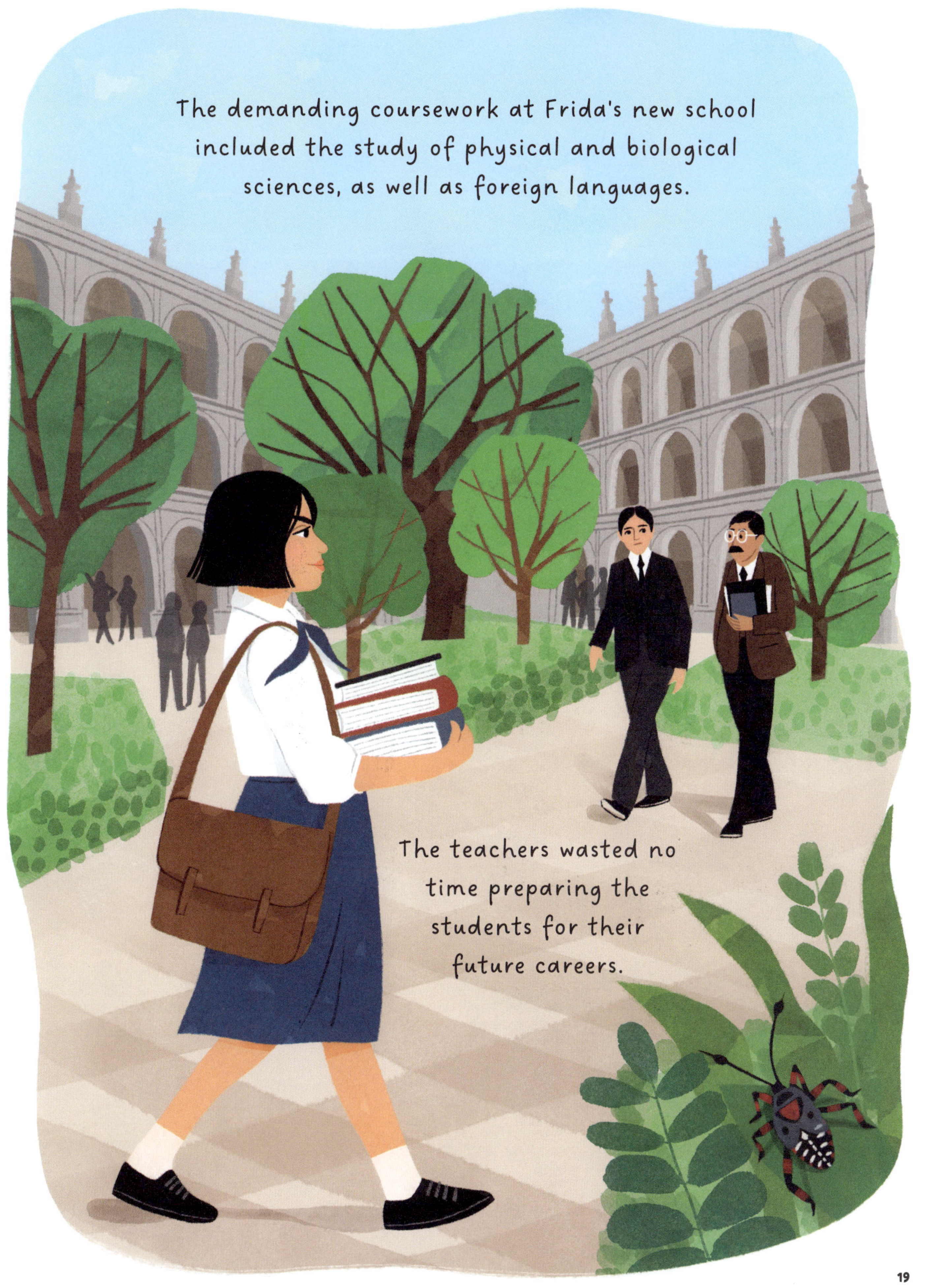

The demanding coursework at Frida's new school included the study of physical and biological sciences, as well as foreign languages.

The teachers wasted no time preparing the students for their future careers.

There were only thirty-five girls among the school's two thousand students, so naturally they all stood out.

Frida debated politics and books with some of them, as well as with a few boys. They called themselves the Cachuchas, the Spanish name for the caps they wore.

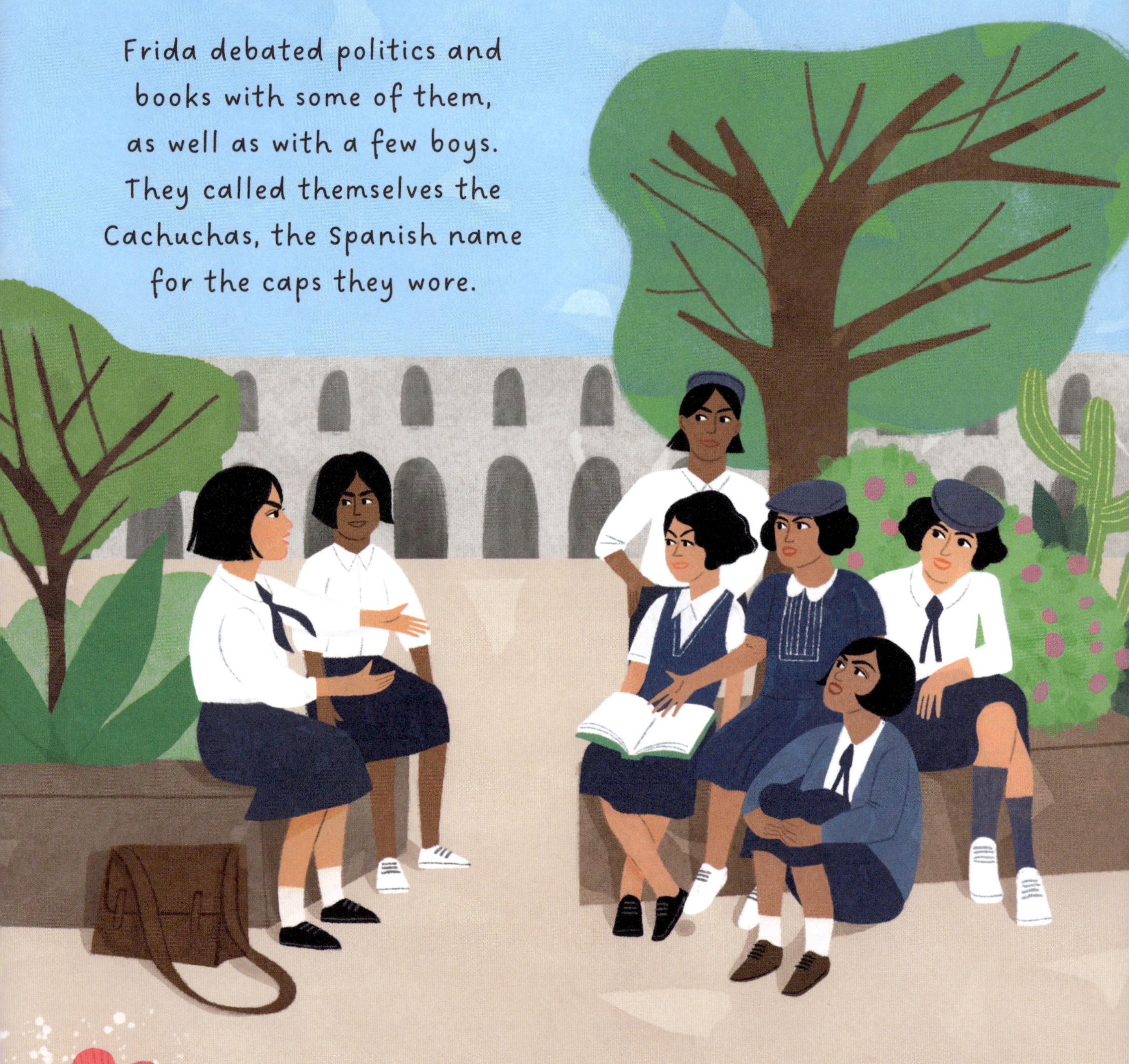

The Cachuchas told jokes and made bold pronouncements about Mexican politics. They wanted to see changes made and were prepared to speak their minds.

Frida's own views were changing, and she could sense this happening on the streets of Mexico, too. People needed more job options and ways to improve their lives.

In her spare time, Frida took on a job working for a commercial painter. It was her first professional experience with art.

Although Frida was busy with her friends and teachers, she couldn't help noticing an artist painting a mural on a large wall behind the school's performing stage.

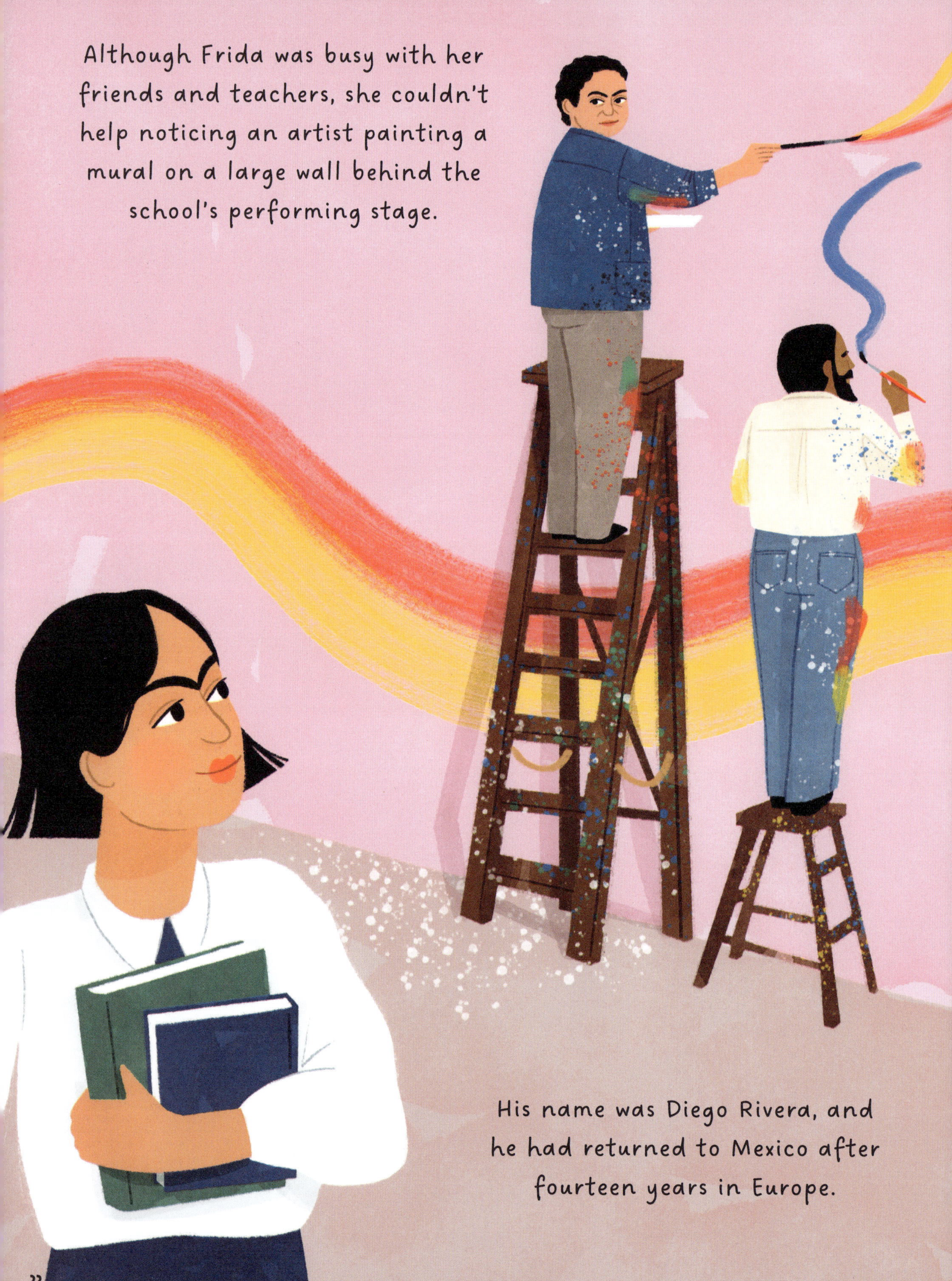

His name was Diego Rivera, and he had returned to Mexico after fourteen years in Europe.

The 36-year-old Rivera was supervising a team of assistants working on a mural called *Creation*. Frida was looking for ways to speak her mind, and Rivera was doing just that through his paintings.

Frida was fascinated by the mural. And something about Diego struck Frida as special.

Outside of school, Frida witnessed violent demonstrations in the streets against the current Mexican government.

Mexico was in a period of social and political upheaval. Old ways were being challenged, but not always without a fight. Women especially wanted more of a voice in governing their own lives, including getting the right to vote.

Frida was not shy about expressing her views supporting these women's rights. She was growing up fast, but maybe not as fast as she would have liked.

Frida had begun to find her voice, and art and politics were equally united forces within it.

The Right to VOTE

Frida was greatly inspired by the political movements that gripped Mexico when she was in her teens—especially women's rights.

Until the 19th century, women's access to education and jobs was severely **limited**. They were expected to stay home and raise families. In most places, they also did not have the right to vote.

Women advocates began to achieve changes in this situation in the 1800s. In the United States, women gained the **right to vote** in 1920. In Great Britain, it was 1928.

But change was slower to come to Mexico, where women did not have the right to vote until 1953.

After the Mexican Revolution ended in 1917, a new government was established. It was more receptive to **women's rights**, partly because women had played an active role in the recent war.

WOMEN ARE CITIZENS

Women were given a **greater role** in politics and granted more educational opportunities. However, these changes were slow to become official.

TRIUMPH OVER TRAGEDY

Frida Finds her Gift

In 1925, when Frida was eighteen, tragedy struck. She was riding on a city bus with her boyfriend from school—Alejandro Gómez Arias.

The bus collided with a trolley car. Frida was thrown from her seat and part of the bus was crushed around her.

Frida was badly injured. Her back was broken in three places. Her right foot had been crushed. The doctors did not know if she would live.

But Frida was strong. After a month in the hospital, she returned home.

Frida was far from healed, though. For several more months she lay in a cast. Almost every movement she took was painful. Even after her life was no longer in danger, Frida did not know if she would ever walk again.

Her recovery was slow. Every day was filled with long, lonely hours.

Luckily, Frida's arms and hands were unharmed. Maybe she could paint.

Her parents made a special easel for her so that she could paint in bed. Frida also had a mirror placed so that she could see herself while she worked.

Painting became the way that Frida escaped her confinement.

At first, she thought she might combine her interest in art and medicine by becoming a medical illustrator.

But her creativity led Frida in new directions. Her brush strokes filled the canvas with her thoughts and emotions.

The more Frida worked, the more she wanted to push the boundaries of her paintings.

Frida also found she could not separate the constant pain she was feeling from her art. So, she didn't try.

Instead, she wove her pain into the way she expressed herself in her painting.

Frida's first painting was a portrait of herself wearing a velvet dress with a detailed collar. It followed in the tradition of 19th-century Mexican portrait painters.

She painted herself because she was often alone, and she felt that she was the subject she knew best. It was an artistic choice that Frida would make again and again, throughout her life.

In this first self-portrait, Frida added a personal touch to her expression. It was not defiant, but it showed a fierce determination.

This was a new Frida, a confident young woman preparing to move forward.

Painting PORTRAITS

Frida became known for her revealing self-portraits. Follow these steps to create your own portraits. Then try to draw a self-portrait, like Frida.

1. When drawing a face, first draw a **circle**.

2. Then draw a **cross** inside the circle. One line from top to bottom, and the other line from side to side.

3. After that, draw a **square** inside the circle that touches the circle in four places.

Now you have reference points for all the facial features.

Add other **details** to give the face a distinctive look or to make it resemble someone you know.

SYMBOLS OF THE PAST

Mixing the Old with the New

Frida was fascinated by Mexico's cultural and physical symbols, and their long history. She was also a different person after a terrible accident, one that would forever leave a mark on her life.

True, Frida had survived. But even after her recovery, she was never completely healed. Her daily life was always marked by pain.

Frida had a choice to make. She could shrink into the background, or she could choose a different course.

Frida was unsure what career she could pursue, given her physical limitations.

She decided to turn her passion to painting. And instead of feeling sorry for herself, Frida began to incorporate her chronic pain and suffering into her art.

At the same time, Frida was more and more caught up with Mexican culture and its history. What made her country distinct? Was it a mixture of fashion and architecture?

How could Frida incorporate these influences into her self-expression? What clothes or jewelry would she choose to wear? And how would these new interests affect her work?

Frida's early paintings were mostly portraits of herself, her family, and her friends. She deliberately evoked a native folk-art style, flattening the perspectives of her subjects. This gave the finished art a deliberately unpolished aspect.

Another new development was that this art was not focused solely on Frida's own experiences.

Frida did not believe in the idea that art should be kept separate from other aspects of everyday life. A painting, she thought, should reflect something of what was going on around its creation.

That "something" could be personal, or it could reflect a movement in society at large.

Frida started to paint watercolors of outdoor scenes in the neighboring town. She also began to add distinctive imagery, like Mexican architectural details and local clothing designs, to her paintings.

The political and social world around Frida was also rapidly changing, and Frida did her best to keep up.

Equal rights for men and women remained an ongoing debate.

In the United States in 1920, a recent law had given women the right to vote. But women in Mexico had no such privilege.

As far as Frida was concerned, men and women should be treated equally.

And so, she made the symbolic decision to wear clothing normally seen on men.

She also stopped removing the hair around her mouth and between her eyebrows. Instead of being embarrassed about these physical traits, she was proud of them.

Frida wanted her life and her art to speak to the traditional culture and new political ideas she cared about.

Symbols of MEXICO

Frida included Mexican symbols representing plants, animals, and skulls in many of her paintings. The symbols stem from the colonial era under Spanish rule, and the more ancient times under the Olmecs, Aztecs, and other native peoples.

Olmec Carved Heads

The Olmecs were the first Mexican civilization, from around 1200–400 BCE (roughly 3,220 years ago). Among the prominent **artifacts** they left behind were carved statues in the shape of heads.

Calavera

The human skull, known as the calavera, was a symbol of the Aztecs, who flourished from 1325 to 1521. It represents **death and rebirth**, marked by the annual Day of the Dead celebrations on November 1 and 2.

Aztec Feathered Serpent

The Aztecs had many artistic symbols in their culture. Feathered serpents, including the creation god **Quetzalcóatl**, were a prominent Aztec symbol.

Aztec Eight-Pointed Star

The Aztecs used an eight-pointed star to represent the **Sun** and the Sun god, Tonatiuh.

Aztec Golden Eagle

The Aztec **golden eagle**, a prominent part of the current Mexican flag, represents bravery and strength.

STORIES IN ART

Frida Finds her Style

In 1928, Frida once again met mural artist Diego Rivera. Given her interest in art, she was drawn to Diego and the cultural circle he traveled in.

Diego was famous, attracting commissions from all over the world. He was used to admirers, but there was something about Frida's intensity that set her apart.

Frida was not shy. She boldly asked for Diego's opinion of her artwork. And he was happy to offer it. The more time they spent together, the stronger their relationship grew.

Finally, they declared their love for each other. Frida's family and friends may have had reservations about the relationship, but she did not. Frida and Diego got married in 1929.

After their wedding, Diego and Frida settled for a time in Cuernavaca, which was several hours away from Mexico City.

There, Diego was working on his latest mural in the 16th century Cortés Palace.

Frida had already begun to refine her personal style. She adopted the bright colors of more traditional Mexican clothing.

Frida stood out in her brightly embroidered blouses and colorful bracelets and necklaces. Her hair was adorned with ribbons. It was a look she adopted from that time on.

Frida's art was also evolving. She realized that a painting was not just a static picture on a canvas. It could combine several distinct elements in a way that a photograph could not.

In the painting *Time Flies* Frida's familiar stern face and figure looks out from the canvas. But an alarm clock sits to her left and an airplane flies in the sky outside. The contrast between Frida's appearance and the objects behind her is striking.

Although Frida is wearing a traditional blouse and a heavy beaded necklace in the painting, both the clock and the plane came from a very different, more modern, period.

They signified that times were changing. Could old traditions adapt to modern needs, and if so, how?

Frida was not declaring that she knew all the answers to these questions. She was experimenting with different ideas about what elements to include in her paintings.

However, Frida did know that she wanted her paintings to do more than simply create an image. Her paintings should tell a story, a story that might reveal intimate details from her personal life.

And these stories might not be happy or pretty ones. If life was making her unhappy—if she and Diego were arguing, for instance—they might be filled with somber or disturbing images.

Part of what made Frida's art unique was that it told the story of her life, in all its light and shade.

Mexican FOLK ART

When Frida started to make Mexican folk art a key part of her artistic style, she was embracing a culture with a long and proud tradition.

Whether in textiles, ceramics, or sculpture, Mexican **craftspeople** have excelled at their work for centuries.

Huipil

The huipil is a colorful **blouse** embroidered with different colors and patterns reflecting the specific area in which it was made.

Rebozo

The rebozo is a **shawl or scarf** that is both practical and fashionable. It can be decorated with different designs depending on the taste of the weaver.

Talavera Pottery

Talavera pottery was introduced by Spanish settlers in the 1500s. It features colorful hand-painted designs on plates, bowls, mugs, and lamps. Talavera **patterns** often draw on pre-Columbian symbols, creating a true mixture of ancient and modern techniques.

Alebrijes

Alebrijes are paper-mache or wooden sculptures, often in the shape of real or imagined **animals**. These brightly colored creatures are a whimsical addition to the sometimes fantastical aspects of Mexican culture.

AN ARTIST WITH PROMISE

Frida Holds her First Solo Show

In November 1930, Frida left her home country of Mexico and traveled to the United States with her husband, mural artist Diego Rivera.

Diego had been offered the job of painting a mural in San Francisco for the San Francisco Stock Exchange. Such commissions were huge, complicated paintings that took months to complete.

Frida took some time adjusting to life in another country. But she found American buildings and landscapes fascinating, and enjoyed standing out for her Mexican clothing.

Ever since being injured in a bus accident aged eighteen, Frida struggled with aches and pains. But she was determined to continue her progress as an artist.

While in San Francisco, Frida heard about the local plant scientist, Luther Burbank. Burbank had developed many crops that had thrived in the California climate.

Frida undertook a large painting of Burbank. It was much more ambitious than her earlier portraits and simple landscapes. She painted him as a commanding figure standing in a farming landscape surrounded by fruits and vines.

This *Portrait of Luther Burbank* is surrealistic, combining realist and fantastical elements together. For example, Burbank's legs become part of the trunk of a tree ending in a visible web of roots.

The effect was both traditional and ground-breaking at the same time.

In 1932, Diego and Frida moved again, this time to Detroit, Michigan, where Diego had another commission to fill.

Diego was consumed by his work, which was hard for Frida. She also missed Mexico. She took these emotionally unsettled feelings and wove them into her paintings.

In one of her longest titled works, *Self Portrait Along the Border Line Between Mexico and The United States*, she showed herself standing between representations of the two countries.

The Mexican half of the painting featured an ancient pyramid and examples of folk art. The American half was about modern industry.

The Frida in the painting holds a Mexican flag in her hand. The United States might be progressive, but it would never be a place she could call home.

As Frida's artistic output was growing, so was her reputation. A few years later, in October 1938, an exhibition of her work opened at a gallery in New York City. It was her first solo show.

Artists, dealers, and members of the public came to see Frida's work. How would her art be received?

The show was a success. Twenty-five of Frida's paintings were on display and half that number were sold. Many people were taking Frida's work as seriously as she did.

Clearly, the New York art world believed in Frida's talent.

MODERN Art

In the 20th century, modern art introduced a new way of presenting images on canvas. People and places were no longer shown in purely realistic depictions. Bold shapes and colors often dominated the paintings.

Artists such as Pablo Picasso (1881–1973) and Henri Matisse (1869–1954) created paintings where **strict realism** was not the goal.

Pablo Picasso

This art resulted in **unexpected** examples of design and perspective.

Henri Matisse

One hundred years later, these new **perspectives** still influence art today.

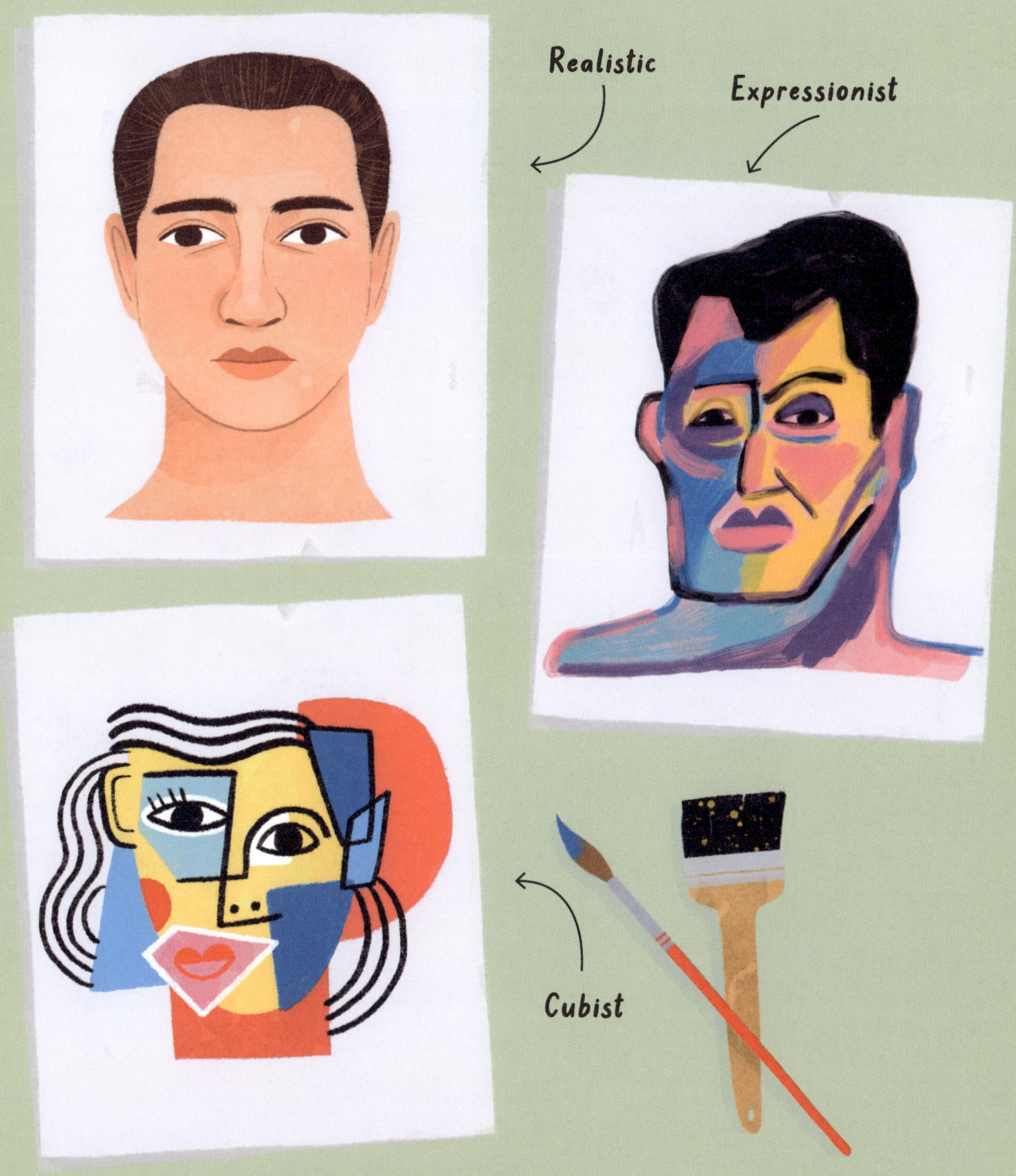

Frida's work did not look like anyone else's—she was stretching the **boundaries** of modern art in her own way.

THE TWO FRIDAS

Frida Doesn't Stray from her Own Path

In March 1939, Frida went to Paris, France, for the exhibition of her first international art show.

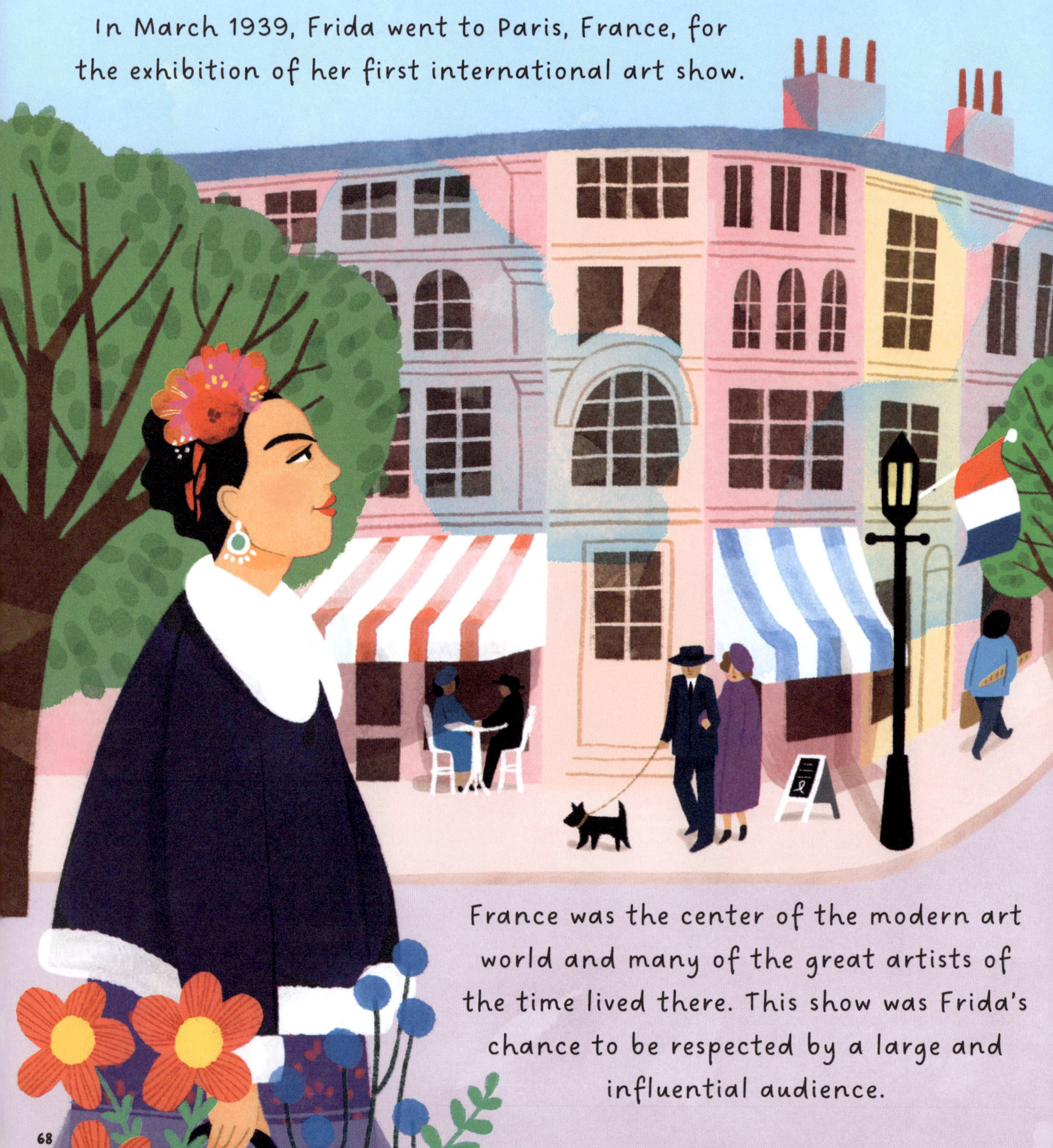

France was the center of the modern art world and many of the great artists of the time lived there. This show was Frida's chance to be respected by a large and influential audience.

These artists often met in studios and cafes to discuss their work. Many of them, including Pablo Picasso and Marc Chagall, came to see Frida's work. And the Louvre, the famous Paris art museum, bought one of her paintings.

Unfortunately, the show was not well-organized. Frida was disappointed that her work was lost in a large exhibit that included many artists. Her art, she believed, had not had the proper chance to shine.

Life at home in Mexico did not make Frida feel any better. Her marriage to Diego Rivera had turned into one argument after another. This friction led them to get divorced, although they remarried the next year.

Frida was taking a hard look at her life. She was thirty-three years old, and her artistic career had not settled into a recognizable path.

Who was the real Frida Kahlo, she wondered? What mattered to her the most?

Out of all this inner wrestling came one of Frida's most important works. It depicts two women, both versions of herself. She called the painting *The Two Fridas.*

The painting has the two Fridas sitting together. The European Frida is on the left and the Mexican Frida is on the right.

The European Frida has an exposed and damaged heart, while the Mexican Frida's heart is whole. The painting shows the two sides of Frida.

The two Fridas are holding hands, suggesting that they are joined—two versions of the same person. However, the stormy clouds behind them suggest that the union is not a happy one.

That storminess represented the uncertain aspects of her life that Frida was trying to hold together. It was unclear what would happen next.

Though they disagreed on many things, Diego had often encouraged Frida when it came to her work.

Frida knew she should adapt her style so that people would hire her to do paintings. But she did not want to give in to this temptation. If other people wanted to buy the art she created, that would be fine. She was more than happy to sell them.

Frida wanted to be an artist on her own terms.

PAINTING *Giants*

In Paris, Frida ended up meeting some of the most famous painters of her age. These artists, like Frida, became public figures known for their broader social views as well as for their artistic work.

Marc Chagall

Marc Chagall (1887–1985) drew his inspiration from modern expressionism, while adding his own distinctive, **dreamlike** sensibility to the mix. He found great success in stained glass as well as his paintings.

Piet Mondrian (1872–1944) favored compositions in **abstract** art that featured grid-like paintings and primary colors. His use of geometric forms made him a champion of Cubism.

Piet Mondrian

Pablo Picasso (1881–1973) could draw in a traditional style but forged a modern artistic path that favored **bold** lines and designs. His mural masterpiece, *Guernica* (1937), revealed his feeling about war.

Pablo Picasso

TEACHING LOS FRIDOS

Frida Shares her Talent

In 1942, Frida took a job teaching at a school called La Esmeralda, in Mexico. However, she was not a typical teacher. She wanted to share her love of art so that the students could pursue their own passions about painting.

The school was a secondary art school run by the Ministry of Education. The students came from working-class families. They did not come from wealthy families with a rich background in art.

Frida had received no training in educating children, and she did not believe that there was only one way to teach art.

Given this approach, it was only natural that her students were not sure what to expect.

Frida didn't leave them in suspense for long. She was enthusiastic about being with the students. She just didn't share any great theories about painting.

Frida treated her students more as equals than as beginners who should learn from her.

Frida's job, as she saw it, was to open her students' eyes to the world. From there, they could choose their own artistic course.

She made a point of sharing her passion for the subject. Frida believed painting was the most terrific thing that there is, but that it required very strict self-discipline and, above all, love.

Frida took her students on field trips to markets and churches.

And all along the way, they discussed literature, sang songs, and listened to musicians on the streets.

One project that Frida arranged was for her students to paint the outer walls of a popular local neighborhood bar, a *pulqueria* called "La Rosita." This name means "The Little Rose."

It was a common practice for crude murals to decorate such walls, and Frida wanted her students to create one of their own based on the bar's name.

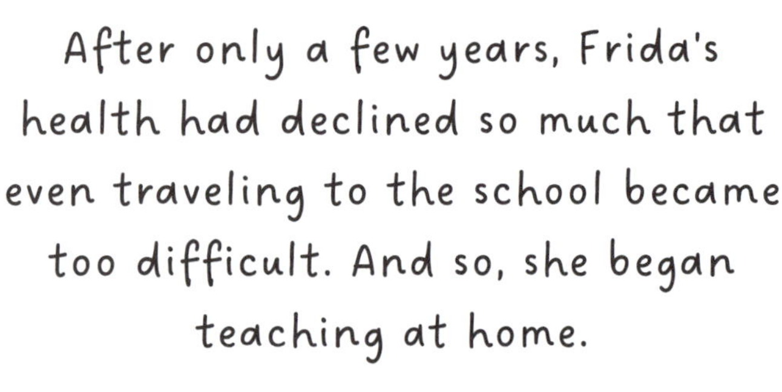

After only a few years, Frida's health had declined so much that even traveling to the school became too difficult. And so, she began teaching at home.

At first, a large number of students made the trip to Frida's house several times a week. Over time, this number fell to a loyal group of four. They became known as Los Fridos.

Her students remembered that she did not want them to be a painter like her. Frida didn't want imitators! She wanted to help open their eyes to the world so that they could become the painters they were meant to be for themselves.

Frida encouraged Los Fridos to develop their own unique styles.

LEARNING from Frida

Even within the world of art, Frida wanted her students to think outside the box. So how did Frida encourage her students to develop their art?

She reminded them of the range of **nature**, from the stars in the night sky to tiny organisms that could only be seen under a microscope.

She encouraged them to read books—not just about art but also works of **literature** and **culture**.

She believed they should do more than study classic art from Europe, the United States, or even Mexico. They should reach back before the colonial eras, before the Renaissance, and become familiar with **pre-Columbian** art and sculpture.

La Esmeralda, where Frida taught, was established in 1927 and still exists today.

THE DEER IN THE WOOD

Balancing Paint and Pain

In the 1940s, Frida's life was a difficult balancing act between her health and her career.

She was in constant pain from injuries she had sustained earlier in her life. Frida had several operations hoping to improve how she felt. She wore a specially constructed corset to give her back additional support.

During Frida's remaining years, she wore a total of twenty-eight different corsets. Some were made of leather or plastic, and one was made of steel. Each was intended to make her daily life a little easier.

But none of these efforts gave her any permanent relief.

"Each day, I am worse," she wrote to her doctor. Even when a corset helped a little, trying to move around in it was exhausting.

In Mexico, Frida had become well known. She was featured in several exhibitions and museums around the country and won a prize from the government. She continued to paint despite the pain she was in.

Among the many styles and looks in an exhibition of mixed artists, there was no mistaking Frida's paintings for the work of anyone else.

Many of her paintings, though, reflected her ongoing discomfort. *The Wounded Deer* shows a deer pierced with many arrows. But in place of the deer's head, Frida painted her own head instead.

The Frida-deer lies wounded in a forest. Frida's face does not look pained, but the deer's body is badly injured. And all around are mostly dead trees without branches or leaves.

Animals found their way into Frida's paintings. Often, they sat in the background or, in the case of monkeys and parrots, resting on her shoulders.

In one self-portrait, one monkey rests on her arm while three others look out just behind her. Frida does not smile at them, but she is clearly content to have them nearby.

Frida also included her favorite dog, the hairless Mr. Xolotl, in several of her paintings. Such dogs had a long history in Mexico, tracing back to the Aztecs, who believed that this breed served the gods.

Beyond the monkeys and parrots, Frida enjoyed the company of three dogs, two turkeys, an eagle, and a fawn. The animals she cared for were a part of her family.

As time passed, Frida spent more time in bed. She had less energy and more pain than ever before. When she did paint, it was only for short periods. But she was not willing to give up. She had learned that people could endure much more than they might think.

She worked on fanciful still lifes, determined to forge ahead in her art.

"I am not sick. I am broken," she wrote in her diary. "But I am happy to be alive as long as I can paint."

Even in her weakened condition, Frida remained committed to creating art.

ANIMALS in Art

People have been drawing or painting animals for as long as they have been drawing anything at all, and they were prominent in Frida's art.

In 1940, four French teenagers discovered drawings of horses and other animals in the **Lascaux Cave** in southwestern France. Some of the pictures are estimated to be up to twenty thousand years old.

In many ancient cultures, animals were used as **symbols**, most notably as examples of good and evil. These images were not meant to be realistic, but they contained recognizable shapes and features.

During the Dutch Golden Age in the 1600s, artists painted **realistic** portraits of animals in natural surroundings.

In modern art, **abstract shapes** and **bold colors** have characterized some pictures of animals, focusing on a specific aspect that sets the animal apart.

FRIDA'S LEGACY

Taking a Final Bow

In her mid-forties, Frida had more and more trouble painting. A lifetime of injuries and illnesses left her in constant pain.

It was getting hard to hold her brush. And even when she could, her fingers shook as she pressed the brush on the canvas.

Her pain also made it difficult to sleep, and without sleep, she could not think clearly. The days ran together in a hazy blur.

But then Frida got some exciting news. In April 1953, she was scheduled to have her first one-woman exhibition in Mexico.

There had never been a solo show of her work near home. Even if she could no longer paint as she once did, Frida looked forward to sharing her earlier paintings with her friends and family.

But Frida's injuries and operations had finally become too much to ignore. Her pain could not be put aside even for a few hours.

She spent much of her time having operations in the hospital and then slowly recovering in bed at home. Sadly, as the number of operations increased, the less successful they were.

At this point, Frida's legs were too weak to support her for any length of time. It would be impossible, her doctor explained, for her to host the opening of her show.

Frida would never be able to stand long enough to greet visitors as they arrived to see her paintings.

But Frida was determined not to miss out. The show was too important. She didn't want to make excuses. She didn't want to cancel.

After some careful thought, Frida made a plan.

She had an ambulance bring her to the show's opening a little early. A wheelchair helped her get inside.

And there, right by the entrance, she lay in her own four-poster bed, which had been brought from home.

Frida remained in bed for the show's opening. There, she welcomed the guests as they arrived. It was almost as if she was part of the exhibition herself!

The crowd was huge. Of course, Frida's friends were there. But there were also many people that admired her work. They were not going to miss the chance to see the great Frida Kahlo one last time.

The crowd was so big that no one spoke to Frida for very long. They were told to keep moving so that everyone there would get the chance to say hello.

The show was a success and an artistic triumph for Frida.

The Reputation of FRIDA KAHLO

Frida was forty-seven when she died in 1954. Her reputation has grown year after year since her death. She is one of the world's most recognizable and influential artists.

Not only is Frida known for her art, but her face, her work, and symbols of her artistic style have graced everything from **T-shirts** to **tea towels**.

Frida has inspired later artists in two distinct ways. First, there is the style of her paintings, the mixing of **surrealistic** scenes with symbols from **Mexican culture** and folklore.

And second, there is her fearless **determination** to incorporate into her paintings the good, the bad, and the ugly from her life. This approach infused her work with a power few other artists could match.

Over her lifetime, Frida produced about two hundred paintings, drawings, and sketches. These works continue to kindle the **imaginations** of artists that have come after her.

MUSEO
FRIDA KAHLO

FRIDA KAHLO'S JOURNEY TO BECOMING A VISIONARY ARTIST

1907

July 6

Frida Kahlo (full name Magdalena Carmen Frida Kahlo Calderón) is **born** in Coyoacán, Mexico.

1913

Frida **becomes ill** with polio and spends nine months recovering in bed.

1922

Frida enters **preparatory school** planning to be a doctor. She later sees the artist Diego Rivera at work on a school mural.

1939

Frida and Diego divorce after years of **arguing**, but then they remarry a year later.

1939

Frida has another art show, this time in **Paris, France**. She meets many famous artists, such as Pablo Picasso and Marc Chagall, but is disappointed in the way her paintings are displayed.

1942

Frida becomes a teacher, but takes a non-traditional approach by exposing her students to **new ideas** rather than just telling them how to paint.

1944

Frida undergoes another in a series of operations to improve her mobility. Most of these operations do not help lessen her **daily pain**.

1925

Frida is badly hurt in a **traffic accident**. While recovering in bed, she takes up painting and considers a change in careers.

1928

Frida meets **Diego Rivera** again. They fall in love and marry the following year.

1930

Frida moves to the United States with Diego for several years as he works on a series of commissions. Her own **art style** continues to evolve.

1938

Frida has her first art show at a gallery in **New York City** and is pleased with the reception to her work.

1953

Frida has her first art show in **Mexico**, which she can only attend by having a bed moved in for her to lie in.

1954

After many long years of **ill health**, Frida dies at the age of 47.